HOW TO USE THIS GUIDE

SCOPE AND SEQUENCE

Welcome to the *40 Days Through the Book* study on the Gospel of Mark. During the course of the next six weeks, you will embark on an in-depth exploration of John Mark's message to the believers in the Church. During this study, you will learn when he wrote the book, the audience for whom it was written, and the context in which it was written. But, more importantly, you will explore the key themes that John Mark relates in the book—and how his teachings apply to you today.

SESSION OUTLINE

The *40 Days Through the Book* video and study guide are designed to be experienced in a group setting (such as a Bible study, Sunday school class, or other small-group gathering) and also as an individual study. Each session begins with an introductory reading and question. You will then watch the video message which can be accessed through streaming by following the instructions printed on the inside front cover. There is an outline provided in the guide for you to take notes and gather your reflections as you watch the video.

Next, you will engage in a time of directed discussion, review the memory verse for the week, and then close each session with a time of prayer. (Note that if you are doing this study with others and the group is larger, you may wish to watch the videos together and then break into smaller groups of four to six people, to ensure that everyone has time to participate in discussions.)

40-DAY JOURNEY

What is truly unique about this study, and the other studies in the *40 Days Through the Book* series, are the daily learning resources that will lead you into a deeper engagement with the text. Each week, you will be given a set of daily readings, with accompanying reflection questions, to help you explore the material that you covered during your group time.

The first day's reading will focus on the key verse to memorize for the week. In the other weekly readings, you will be invited to read a passage from the Gospel of Mark, reflect on the text, and then respond with some guided journal questions. On the final day, you will review the key verse again and recite it from memory. As you work through the six weeks' worth of material in this section, you will read (and, in some cases, reread) the entire book of Mark.

Now, you may be wondering why you will be doing this over the course of *forty* days. Certainly, there is nothing special about that number. But there is something biblical about it. In the Bible, the number forty typically designates a time of *testing*. Noah was in the ark for forty days. Moses lived forty years in Egypt and another forty years in the desert before he

STUDY GUIDE + STREAMING VIDEO
SIX SESSIONS

MARK

IN THE COMPANY OF CHRIST

JEFF MANION

with KEVIN & SHERRY HARNEY

HarperChristian
Resources

CONTENTS

led God's people. He spent forty days on Mount Sinai receiving God's laws and sent spies, for forty days, to investigate the land of Canaan. Later, God sent the prophet Jonah to warn ancient Nineveh, for forty days, that its destruction would come because of the people's sins.

Even more critically, in the New Testament we read that Jesus spent forty days in the wilderness, fasting and praying. It marked a critical transition point in his ministry—the place where he set about to fulfill the mission that God had intended. During this time Jesus was tested relentlessly by the enemy . . . and prevailed. When he returned to Galilee, he was a different person than the man who had entered into the wilderness forty days before. The same will be true for you as you commit to this forty-day journey through Mark.

GROUP FACILITATION

If you are doing this study with others, you and your fellow group members should have your own copy of this study guide. Not only will this help you engage when your group is meeting, but it will also allow you to fully enter into the *40 Days* learning experience. Keep in mind the video, questions, and activities are simply tools to help you engage with the session. The real power and life-transformation will come as you dig into the Scriptures and seek to live out the truths you learn along the way.

You will need to appoint a leader or facilitator for the group who is responsible for starting the video teaching and for keeping track of time during discussions and activities. Leaders may also read questions aloud and monitor discussions, prompting participants to respond and ensuring that everyone has the opportunity to participate. For more thorough instructions on this role, see the Leader's Guide included at the back of this guide.

INTRODUCTION

MARK

AUTHOR, DATE, AND LOCATION

John Mark was not one of the original disciples of Jesus. His name first appears in the book of Acts, after Peter miraculously escaped from prison and made his way to a home that belonged to John Mark's mother (see Acts 12:12). From there, the young man became a traveling companion of Paul and Barnabas, until he deserted them in Pamphylia, causing a rift between the two men (see 12:25; 13:13; 15:39). John Mark went on to travel with Barnabas, but scholars believe he maintained a close association with Peter, from whom he learned about the Savior. John Mark penned his fast-paced Gospel just a few decades after the death and resurrection of Jesus, in the early AD 60s, to believers in Rome and around the Roman world. This was a time of severe persecution, and his Gospel brought hope to those who were feeling discouraged. It also gave clarity for anyone who wondered what it meant to be a follower of Jesus.

THE BIG PICTURE

While the three other Gospel writers—Matthew, Luke, and John—focused on details of Jesus' birth, life, death, and resurrection, Mark gets right to the heart of the matter. A few decades had passed since Jesus' ministry, and some people were growing a bit fuzzy about what it meant to be a follower of the Messiah. Persecution of Christians was intensifying, and there was a temptation among the believers to compromise, apologize, or simply give up on their faith. Sadly, some were doing exactly that!

So, Mark needed to take the early Christians back to the basics. With clarity and precise language, he pulls no punches as he explains exactly what it means to be a follower of Christ. As we read his words, we discover an invitation to ask: *Who is this Jesus? What does he expect of me? Is suffering a normal part of the Christian life? What will encourage and strengthen my trust in Jesus?* These are questions that all who put their faith in Jesus—at some point in their lives—will ask themselves, maybe again and again. These questions are not born of a lack of faith but serve to strengthen and stabilize our relationship with the Savior.

As we read John Mark's rapid-fire account of the ministry of Jesus, we find answers to these questions . . . and many others. When we embrace these biblical answers, our faith will solidify, our hope will deepen, and our pathway forward will grow clear. We fill find that God's strength fills us as Jesus draws near. So lace up your running shoes. Open your heart and mind. And come with your questions! Get ready to move as Mark's Gospel reveals what it means to follow Jesus. Your life will never be the same.

EPIC THEMES

There are several themes in Romans that are worthy of our focus. Some of these include:

- **Jesus has been given all authority.** This authority was clear for everyone to see. Jesus had power over the natural world, spiritual forces, sickness, and even death. As people encountered the Savior and recognized this, they were either drawn to him or resisted him (see Mark 1–3).

- **Jesus calls us and sends us out.** There were many people who flooded to Jesus and were drawn to his ministry. But out of the many, Jesus called twelve men to be with him and to go out with his message to the world. Jesus calls people near to him, and then he sends them out (see Mark 3–6).

- **Jesus was always willing to reveal God's truth.** Even those who walked closest to Jesus and witnessed his power, ministry, and character did not fully understand who he was or what he expected of them. Although many others seemed to be deaf to the truth of God and blind to who he was, Jesus was always ready to open ears and give sight to the blind (see Mark 6–8).

- **Jesus redefined greatness.** Jesus told his followers that he would suffer and die. He also declared on multiple occasions that after he died, he would rise from the grave. He wanted his followers to understand that humble service was the path of discipleship. Greatness is found in following him and walking the path of sacrifice (see Mark 8–10).

- **Jesus is the King of heaven and ruler of an eternal kingdom.** Near the end of Jesus' life, as he came to Jerusalem, he presented himself as the King. The crowds celebrated this declaration, but the religious leaders challenged his authority at every turn and eventually had him put to death (see Mark 11–13).

- **Jesus rose from the grave.** Jesus, the servant King, was arrested, mocked, abused, tried, crucified, and executed on a cross. He was placed in a tomb and was dead for three days. But then he rose again in glory, power, and eternal authority over hell, death, and the grave. Jesus is still the King of all kings and rules today and for eternity (see Mark 14–16).

Those who prefer a slow and ambling journey through the life of Jesus that fills in every blank and has a flourish on every sentence will struggle with Mark's Gospel. But those who love to get to the point, who prefer direct communication, and who appreciate it when others tell it like it is, will delight in Mark's approach. So, as you start this journey, take a deep breath, say a prayer, and get ready to move at the rapid pace of Mark's Gospel.

THE INVITATION

MARK 1:1–3:6

In the opening chapters of Mark, we see the meteoric rise of Jesus. We then witness conflict when the religious leaders decide they do not like what Jesus is teaching and how the crowds are drawn to him. Jesus is helping the people of his day understand who he is and what he expects of those who make the decision to follow him.

WELCOME

When expectations are crystal clear, everyone benefits. Just consider the workplace. Employers who give their new employees a written job description with detailed responsibilities and expectations avoid all kinds of future problems. Just imagine a boss telling a brand-new employee, "We don't have job descriptions or specific responsibilities for our employees. We just hope you figure things out as you go!" It would be a recipe for disaster.

1

Likewise, couples repeat vows at their wedding ceremony to set up clear expectations. The couple vows to stick together and love each other "in sickness and in health, for better and for worse," for as long as they both shall live. We have all heard these words at weddings. Why do they matter? Because any significant commitment involves setting up clear expectations and declarations of how the parties will conduct themselves.

In our modern world, we often end up skimming over words of commitment and rashly clicking the approve button. Just think about those agreements or contracts that pop up on a computer or tablet. When was the last time you actually *read* every word in these agreements? Most of us just scroll to the end and click "agree" without a second thought.

In the Gospel of Mark, we find that Jesus gave us clear expectations about *who he was* and *what he expects of us.* When it comes to following Jesus, we are wise to slow down and read the fine print. There is nothing better than being a disciple of Jesus, but there is also nothing that will call us to greater commitment and sacrifice.

So, as you begin this study, pay close attention to the words of this powerful biography of Jesus. It will reveal who Jesus is with staggering precision. It will also show who you are to be and what is expected if you are going to bear his name and accept the call to follow him.

SHARE

Think about when you first made the decision to follow Jesus. What did you think was expected of a Christian? How has your understanding changed and matured over time?

WATCH

Watch the video for session one. (Play the DVD or see the instructions on the inside front cover on how to access the sessions through streaming.) As you watch, use the following outline to record any thoughts or concepts that stand out to you.

Background information on Mark's Gospel

Two key questions in the Gospel of Mark:

Who is Jesus?

What does he want?

John the Baptist prepares the way (Mark 1:2–8)

Jesus is introduced (Mark 1:9–13)

Calling the first disciples—a mission of "kingdom expansion" (Mark 1:16–20)

Jesus' growing popularity (Mark 1:21–45)

Growing tensions with the religious establishment:

Conflict over **forgiveness of sins** (Mark 2:1–12)

Conflict over **friendships** (Mark 2:13–17)

Conflict over **fasting** (Mark 2:18–22)

Conflict over **working on the Sabbath** (Mark 2:23–28)

Conflict over **healing on the Sabbath** (Mark 3:1–6)

DISCUSS

Take a few minutes with your group members to discuss what you just watched and explore these concepts in Scripture. Use the following questions to help guide your discussion.

1. What impacted you the most as you watched Jeff's teaching on Mark 1:1–3:6?

2. **Read Mark 1:2–3, 7–8, 10–11, 24, and 27.** What do you learn about who Jesus is as you read these passages from a variety of different perspectives? How would you respond if a non-believing friend asked you, "Who is Jesus?"

3. **Read Mark 1:16–20.** When did you first accept the invitation to follow Jesus? How have you tried to live out the expectations that Jesus lays out in this passage?

4. The people of Jesus' day were amazed at his authority. In the opening chapter of Mark, we read how Jesus had power over demonic forces (see 1:21–28), illnesses (see verses 29–34), and relationships between people (see verses 40–45). How have you seen Jesus set a person free from the influence of sin? How have you seen Jesus bring healing into a person's life? How have you seen Jesus heal a broken relationship?

5. **Read Mark 2:1–12.** Why were the religious leaders so upset that Jesus declared this man to be forgiven of his sins? Why does Jesus have the authority to forgive sins?

6. **Read Mark 2:13–17.** In the first century, a Rabbi would never have been seen sharing intimate table fellowship with tax collectors and "sinners." What do you learn about Jesus as you read this passage? What are some ways you can follow his example when it comes to helping broken and lost people encounter the love and grace of God?

MEMORIZE

Each session, you will be given a key verse (or verses) from the passage covered in the video teaching to memorize. This week, your memory verses are from Mark 1:16–17:

> *As Jesus walked beside the Sea of Galilee, he saw Simon and his brother Andrew casting a net into the lake, for they were fishermen. "Come, follow me," Jesus said, "and I will send you out to fish for people."*

Have everyone recite these verses out loud. Then go around the room again and have everyone try to say them completely from memory.

RESPOND

What will you take away from this session? What is a practical next step you can take in the coming week as you seek to understand Jesus' expectations of his disciples?

PRAY

Close your group time by praying in any of the following directions:

- Pray for the Holy Spirit to help you learn more about who Jesus is as you walk through the Gospel of Mark together during the coming sessions.
- Ask Jesus to fill you with power to live in ways that fulfill his desires and expectations of his disciples.
- Praise Jesus for his amazing authority over all things and ask him to unleash that power in your life, home, church, and community.

SESSION ONE

Reflect on the material you have covered in this session by engaging in the following between-session learning resources. Each week, you will begin by reviewing the key verses to memorize for the session. During the next five days, you will have an opportunity to read a portion of Mark, reflect on what you learn, respond by taking action, journal some of your insights, and pray about what God has taught you. Finally, on the last day, you will again review the key verses and reflect on what you have learned for the week.

DAY 1

Memorize: Begin this week's personal study by reciting Mark 1:16–17:

> As Jesus walked beside the Sea of Galilee, he saw Simon and his brother Andrew casting a net into the lake, for they were fishermen. "Come, follow me," Jesus said, "and I will send you out to fish for people."

Now try to say these verses completely from memory.

Reflect: John Mark tells a story of *good news* from the beginning to the end of his Gospel. Jesus, the Savior, has come. He is God's beloved Son, and his kingdom is breaking into human history. Whether you are a new believer or a long-time follower of Christ, what good news have you experienced because of your relationship with the Lord? How do you express your thankfulness that God has brought this good news?

DAY 2

Read: Mark 1:1–15.

Reflect: This section of Mark begins and ends with the words "good news." Mark starts by telling the world that the "good news" begins with Jesus the Messiah. Just fifteen verses later, we hear Jesus proclaim the "good news." In his own words, he declares, "The kingdom of God has come near. Repent and believe the good news" (verse 15). The coming of Jesus is good news in every way possible. How is Jesus the source of good news in the world and in your life? What are some ways you can share the good news of Jesus with people around you who live in a world saturated with bad news?

Journal:
- What were some of the conditions in the world at the time Mark wrote his Gospel that made good news so needed and welcomed?
- What are some things in our world today that make the good news of Jesus stand out?

Pray: Thank Jesus for leaving heaven, entering our world, and bringing good news to every person who will receive what he has to offer.

DAY 3

Read: Mark 1:16–28.

Reflect: Jesus' invitation was simple but powerful: "Follow me." All four of the men Jesus invited to be his disciples freely left their careers and began a new life. They stopped fishing with nets and began to fish for people. They followed their Rabbi, Jesus, and walked with him, traveled where he went, learned from his teaching, and became like their leader. What have you left behind so that you could follow Jesus and engage in his plan for your life? What do you still need to lay down and surrender so that you can fully live for Jesus?

Journal:
- How has it felt to leave things behind, make sacrifices, and surrender your will for the sake of Jesus?
- What is one thing that you are having a hard time letting go? What step can you take to lay this down and follow Jesus with greater abandon?

Pray: Ask God to give you wisdom to see what still needs to be laid down and left behind as you follow Jesus. Pray for the courage to follow Jesus no matter the cost or the sacrifice.

DAY 4

Read: Mark 1:29–45.

Reflect: This section of Mark starts with an intense day of ministry where Jesus heals, leads a revival meeting, and casts out demons. It ends with Jesus healing a man with leprosy. In the middle of this action, Jesus slips away early in the morning to find a quiet place so he can talk with his Father. He takes a walk in the dark, finds a solitary place, and prays. It seems the more intense life became, the more Jesus needed to be in the presence of the Father. How does busyness and an intense schedule impact your prayer life? What can you do to make space to pray and meet with Jesus on a regular basis?

Journal:
- What are some of the habits, patterns, and disciplines you have developed that have helped you better connect with God?
- What experiences in your day seem to push you away from God? How can you make space to meet with God during those times?

DAY 5

Read: Mark 2:1–17.

Reflect: There are many characters in this story. As always, Jesus is central. But as you read this story, pay special attention to the religious leaders (the teachers of the law). These are religious professionals. As Jesus is speaking, they ask themselves a great question: "Who can forgive sins but God alone?" (verse 7). The answer is important: "No one!" Only God can forgive sins. But this is Jesus' point. He is God, fully divine, the Almighty One! Mark asks this question—"who is Jesus?"—again and again in his Gospel. Our Savior gives an answer in this passage . . . He is God! How has Jesus extended forgiveness to you as you walk with him each day? How will you pray for those in your life who need to know the forgiveness they long for is found in Christ?

Journal:
- As you think about this passage, what were the religious leaders right about? What were the religious leaders wrong about?
- Since Jesus is divine and fully God, how should this view the way you think about him, worship him, and follow him?

Pray: Lift up praise to Jesus as God Almighty, your Creator, and the One who paid the full price so that your sins could be washed away.

DAY 6

Read: Mark 2:18–3:6.

Reflect: There is a lot of intensity and emotion in this passage. A man with a physical ailment needs healing. The religious leaders are suspicious of Jesus and seeking to accuse him of breaking their laws. Jesus is deeply concerned for the man and cares about his condition. When he asks the religious leaders about the appropriateness of healing the man right then and there—on the *Sabbath*—they stay silent and stubborn. Jesus is angry and deeply distressed at the condition of their hearts. For them, religion had become more important than people.

At the end of the passage, Jesus heals the man. This should have brought joy to everyone—including the religious leaders. But they were so upset at Jesus breaking their rules that they want to have him executed. What are some ways religious rules and observances can actually get in the way of following Jesus? Are there any religious rituals, rules, or observances that are a roadblock to you following the Savior?

Journal:
- What are some of the man-made rules and regulations that can get in the way of following Jesus?

- In what ways do you need to focus more on your Savior and less on human regulations?

Pray: Thank Jesus for loving people more than upholding religious traditions. Pray for your heart and life to mirror his example of compassion and action that sets people free.

DAY 7

Memorize: Conclude this week's personal study by again reciting Mark 1:16–17:

> As Jesus walked beside the Sea of Galilee, he saw Simon and his brother Andrew casting a net into the lake, for they were fishermen. "Come, follow me," Jesus said, "and I will send you out to fish for people."

Now try to say these verses completely from memory.

Reflect: Come follow me! Go out and live for me! This was Jesus' call to his first disciples—and his call to us today. What does it mean for you to follow Jesus in the flow of a normal day? What are some ways that you sense Jesus is calling you to go out and live for him?

LESSONS FOR DISCIPLES

MARK 3:7–5:54

*Jesus trained his disciples to trust him,
no matter what they faced. When we know who
Jesus is, we will trust him. When we trust him,
we can follow him anywhere he leads.*

WELCOME

It takes time to build trust. In many cases, it can take months or even years. But it only takes a *moment* for trust to be shattered. One promise broken, an irresponsible action, a harsh word . . . and everything can change. Trust is essential in every relationship in your life. Intimacy and relational health comes when you believe in others' words and count on their promises.

Consider a marriage relationship. A marriage built on trust is a beautiful thing to behold. When a man and woman enter this covenant, they promise to be trustworthy to one another. As years pass and each one upholds their vows and honors the other person, joy and hope fill their relationship. This is God's desire, and he delights when two people become one and can trust the other with no reservation.

Or consider a friendship where both parties speak with honesty, follow through on commitments, and support each other. When friends show up during the hard times of life to share sorrows and support each other, trust is forged. When those same people sincerely rejoice in the good moments and delight in each other's successes, both of them feel a confidence in the relationship that is cherished.

Or think about a work or church relationship. When employees know that their boss is as good as his or her word and will always follow through, they feel secure and at peace. When pastors speak the truth to their congregations and act on what they say with conviction and consistency, that church can thrive. Every relationship is strengthened by trust.

In the same way, when we know who Jesus is, we can trust his plans, his leading, and his call on our life. As our trust in him grows, we will follow him with growing confidence and peace.

SHARE

Think about a person in your life who has been consistently trustworthy. How has your trust in that person impacted the way you respond to what he or she says and asks of you?

WATCH

Watch the video for session two. (Play the DVD or see the instructions on the inside front cover on how to access the sessions through streaming.) As you watch, use the following outline to record any thoughts or concepts that stand out to you.

Jesus chooses the twelve disciples (Mark 3:13–19)

Opposition to Jesus continues (Mark 3:20–35)

The parable of the sower and the soils (Mark 4:1–20)

Other parables of the kingdom of God (Mark 4:26–34)

Four previews of God's coming kingdom:

Power over nature: Jesus calms a storm (Mark 4:35–41)

Power over darkness: Jesus frees a demon-possessed man (Mark 5:1–20)

Power over disease: Jesus heals a woman (Mark 5:25–34)

Power over death: Jesus raises a girl (Mark 5:21–24, 35–43)

Who is Jesus and why should we trust him?

DISCUSS

Take time with your group members to discuss what you just watched and explore these concepts in Scripture. Use the following questions to help guide your discussion.

1. What impacted you the most as you watched Jeff's teaching on Mark 3:7–5:54?

2. Jesus called the disciples to be with him (see Mark 3:14). What did that look like in their lives? What does it look like for Christians to "be with Jesus" in our modern world? What are some ways that you seek to "be with Jesus"?

3. **Read Mark 3:30–35.** How did Jesus redefine what it meant to be a family? What was he communicating to his followers? If you embraced Jesus' teaching in this passage, how might it change the way you engage with other believers in the church?

4. **Read Mark 4:1–20.** Jesus was clear that people respond in a variety of ways when they hear the good news of God's kingdom. What are the four ways that Jesus described? How do you see evidence of each of these types of responses in the world today?

5. **Read Mark 4:35–41.** What did the disciples learn about Jesus in this passage? When was a time that Jesus delivered you from a storm or difficult situation in your life? How did the experience expand your trust in the Savior?

6. Before Jesus raised a young girl to life, he said to the people who had gathered to mourn, "Don't be afraid; just believe" (Mark 5:36). When were some times that Jesus called you to exercise your faith in what seemed to be hopeless situations? What did you learn from the experiences?

MEMORIZE

Your memory verses for this week are from Mark 3:31–32:

> *[The kingdom of God] is like a mustard seed, which is the smallest of all seeds on earth. Yet when planted, it grows and becomes the largest of all garden plants, with such big branches that the birds can perch in its shade.*

Have everyone recite these verses out loud. Then go around the room again and have everyone try to say them completely from memory.

RESPOND

All throughout this section of Mark's Gospel, we discover that Jesus has authority over *everyone* and *everything* on this earth and in the spiritual realm. What is one area of your life you need to surrender fully to the authority of Jesus? How can the members pray for you and support you in your effort to live under the authority of Jesus in this specific area?

PRAY

Close your group time by praying in any of the following directions:

- Thank Jesus for his authority over sickness, nature, evil, and the grave. Ask him to grow your trust in his ability to take care of whatever you face.
- Pray for someone you know who is battling some kind of illness, emotional turmoil, or relational challenge. Ask Jesus to draw near and show his glory and power in this situation.
- Ask the Holy Spirit to lead you wherever the Father wants to take you. Commit to follow him with a humble and surrendered heart.

SESSION TWO

Reflect on the material you have covered in this session by engaging in the following between-session learning resources. Each week, you will begin by reviewing the key verses to memorize for the session. During the next five days, you will have an opportunity to read a portion of Mark, reflect on what you learn, respond by taking action, journal some of your insights, and pray about what God has taught you. Finally, on the last day, you will again review the key verses and reflect on what you have learned for the week.

DAY 8

Memorize: Begin this week's personal study by reciting Mark 3:31–32:

> [The kingdom of God] is like a mustard seed, which is the smallest of all seeds on earth. Yet when planted, it grows and becomes the largest of all garden plants, with such big branches that the birds can perch in its shade.

Now try to say these verses completely from memory.

Reflect: The people of Jesus' day were familiar with the mustard plant, which sprouted from a small seed but quickly grew to a shrub of three to four feet high. Once rooted it spread quickly and often overtook the other plants in the area. Why do you think Jesus used this metaphor to describe the kingdom of God? What does this tell you about what God's kingdom is like?

DAY 9

Read: Mark 3:7–34.

Reflect: Jesus called the twelve disciples to do two things: (1) be with him, and (2) go out and share his message with the world. Notice the order: first be with Jesus, and *then* go out on his behalf. What a lesson for each of us! Think about the flow of your life. Are you making space to be with Jesus—to sit at his feet, to feast on his Word, to talk with him in prayer? If not, what can you do to spend time with Jesus more consistently?

Journal:
- What are the places, activities, or disciplines that help you feel closest to Jesus?
- What gets in the way of you spending time with Jesus? How can you remove some of those obstacles?

Pray: Ask for growing discipline to make time to be with Jesus each day. Pray that you will experience delight in the presence of Jesus that will draw you closer to him.

DAY 10

Read: Mark 4:1–20.

Reflect: The farmer in this parable is reckless and generous. He scatters seed everywhere! In the ancient world, most farmers were poor and lived from harvest to harvest. They would not throw seed in the weeds or on a path—it was too expensive. But the farmer in Jesus' story throws seed everywhere. What lesson can you take from the practices of the farmer in this parable? Where can you scatter the seed of God's Word with greater generosity?

Journal:
- Where are some places that God puts you in the flow of a normal week in which you can encounter people who are in different places spiritually?
- What are some creative and natural ways that you can scatter the seed of God's Word, truth, and gospel as you travel through an ordinary day?

Pray: Ask God to bring a great harvest through the seeds you scatter this coming week.

DAY 11

Read: Mark 4:21–34.

Reflect: Sometimes Jesus said things that seemed baffling or hard to understand. One such declaration is when our Savior said, "Whoever has will be given even more; whoever does not have, even what they have will be taken from them" (verse 25). If we remove this from the context of the Gospels, his words can seem harsh and heartless. But when we understand that Jesus said a lot about stewardship and the importance of his followers using what they have for his glory, we recognize something more is happening here.

Jesus delights in those who are generous—and he gives them more so they can *keep* being generous. He rejoices when we use our spiritual gifts to edify the Church and impact the world. This is not a passage about God being unkind to those who have little. Rather, it is about how God responds to those who take the little they have and use it strategically for his glory. What has God placed in your hands, heart, and life (material goods, abilities, spiritual gifts) that you can invest and use for his glory? What is one way you can be generous and more intentional in the use of your gifts for the sake of Christ?

Journal:
- What helps you to be generous and share what you have with others?
- What gets in the way of you being generous with your resources, time, and abilities? How can you avoid those roadblocks?

Pray: Ask God to help you see your material resources, abilities, and spiritual gifts as things to share freely and joyfully.

DAY 12

Read: Mark 4:35–5:20.

Reflect: What a study in contrasts! A storm is pounding the boat, and the disciples (a number of them seasoned fishermen) are certain the boat will sink. Jesus, on the other hand, is sleeping soundly in the stern. He is so deep in sleep that disciples have to wake him up and explain the situation. "Quiet! Be still!" Just a few words from the Savior, and the wind dies down and everything is calm. Jesus rebukes the disciples for their fear and lack of faith.

Now, here is the humorous part. Notice how they responded to Jesus' authority over the storm and created world: "They were terrified" (Mark 4:41). They were distraught over the storm—and now they are terrified over the power of Jesus, wondering who he could be. When have you been ruled by fear, even when Jesus was right there with you? How can you take hold of your faith in those kinds of moments and trust that Jesus has the authority over all?

Journal:

- What are the moments in life—the situations you face—that cause you the most fear, anxiety, or terror?
- How can you focus more intensely on Jesus during those moments and draw courage from the fact that he is with you and has power over whatever you face?

Pray: Ask the Holy Spirit to help you focus your eyes, heart, and mind on Jesus every time you begin to feel fear or worry creep into your heart.

DAY 13

Read: Mark 5:21–43.

Reflect: Much of Jesus' ministry happened as he was going from one place to another. In this passage, Jesus is traveling to the home of Jairus, a synagogue leader whose little daughter was dying. You can imagine the urgency of the situation. But along the way, a woman reached out, touched Jesus' cloak, and was healed. Jesus paused instead of pressing on and looked for the woman. He affirmed her and sent her off with a blessing of peace. What do you learn from Jesus' willingness to stop, engage, and care for the woman in this situation?

Journal:
- When are you tempted to move too fast and possibly go past opportunities to care, love, and share the grace of Jesus with a person in need?
- How could you seek to slow down so you can notice and respond to the needs your Lord might place right in front of you?

Pray: Ask God to help you slow down and recognize when there is a person in your life who needs a touch from him. Pray for the patience to stop and respond as you feel Jesus would have you do.

DAY 14

Memorize: Conclude this week's personal study by again reciting Mark 3:31–32:

> *[The kingdom of God] is like a mustard seed, which is the smallest of all seeds on earth. Yet when planted, it grows and becomes the largest of all garden plants, with such big branches that the birds can perch in its shade.*

Now try to say these verses completely from memory.

Reflect: Worldly kingdoms come and go, but God's kingdom will never end. It is growing . . . and growing . . . and growing. As a follower of Jesus, you are part of God's plan to transform the world. What can you do to engage in God's plan to bring his will, ways, and kingdom on earth as it is in heaven? What action can you take to show others that God is at work in the world?

HEARING AND SEEING

MARK 6:1–8:26

A fresh way to look at Jesus is to study his disciples as they walked with him and watched his actions. Sometimes they heard his words clearly and understood what he was doing. At other times they completely missed the point of what Jesus was doing in their midst. If we are honest, we likewise all have a lot to learn about hearing, seeing, and following our Savior.

WELCOME

The father and mother of a toddler called the police in a panic when they could not find their son. They had looked everywhere, scoured the house, and checked in with the neighbors. For almost an hour, the parents, police, and neighbors joined in the search. Then, to the parents' utter shock, they found the missing toddler. He was sleeping on the couch right in their living room! He had snuggled into a quilt that was the same color as his pajamas and fallen into a deep sleep. No one noticed him lying there.

How could the parents have not seen the one they were looking for right in front of them? Well, have you ever hunted for a pair of glasses and found them on top of your head? Have you looked in your purse three times for a missing set of keys and finally found them on the fourth time? Do you remember a time when you asked a friend a question and he or she looked at you and said, "I already told you . . . three times!"

Sometimes, we don't see what is in plain sight. There are moments when we don't hear what was clearly spoken to us. We can miss things, be distracted, or simply not get it.

As we study Mark, we learn the disciples also had moments when they missed what was right in front of them. They heard what Jesus said but did not understand his words. They saw what he did, but the deeper truths did not sink in. Jesus was patient, but he wanted his disciples to hear fully, see clearly, open their hearts, and understand what he wanted to do in this world. He wants the same of his followers today.

SHARE

Think about a time when something was right in front of you but somehow you missed it. What was the situation? What caused you to miss seeing it even though it was in plain sight?

WATCH

Watch the video for session three. (Play the DVD or see the instructions on the inside front cover on how to access the sessions through streaming.) As you watch, use the following outline to record any thoughts or concepts that stand out to you.

Sending out the Twelve (Mark 6:7–13)

Feeding the 5,000 (Mark 6:30–44)

Jesus walks on the water (Mark 6:45–52)

The Syrophoenician woman (Mark 7:24–30)

Healing the deaf man (Mark 7:31–37)

Feeding the 4,000 (Mark 8:1–21)

A blind man sees Jesus (Mark 8:22–26)

DISCUSS

Take a few minutes with your group members to discuss what you just watched and explore these concepts in Scripture. Use the following questions to help guide your discussion.

1. What impacted you the most as you watched Jeff's teaching on Mark 6:1–8:26?

2. Jesus sent out his first disciples traveling light. He said, "Take nothing for the journey except . . ." and then gave a short list of what to bring (Mark 6:8). Why do you think Jesus called his disciples to refrain from packing all the things

they might have been tempted to bring? What lesson did he want them to learn from this instruction?

3. Jesus sometimes places his followers in situations where they don't have everything they need so they can learn to depend on his provision, wisdom, and leading. Think about an area of your life where you don't have all you need to accomplish what must be done. How is Jesus leading, guiding, and providing for you through this season?

4. **Read Mark 6:47–52.** Mark writes that when Jesus stepped into the boat after walking on the water, his disciples "were completely amazed, for they had not understood about the loaves; their hearts were hardened" (verses 51–52). What was the lesson of the loaves? Why was it so important for the disciples (and for us) to learn this lesson?

5. **Read Mark 8:14–21.** After Jesus feeds the 4,000, it is clear the disciples have been deaf to his teaching and blind to his power to provide. So Jesus unleashes a rapid-fire series of questions during a trip with them across the lake. What was Jesus trying to get them to understand? Why is it important for us to also learn these things?

6. **Read Mark 8:22–26.** Jesus' healing of a blind man in this passage involves a process in which Christ prays for the man two times. In the same way, the disciples are gaining their "spiritual" sight through a gradual process. Think about your own journey of faith. What has helped you move forward in this gradual process of seeing and hearing what God is communicating to you?

MEMORIZE

Your memory verses for this week are from Mark 6:7–8:

Calling the Twelve to him, he began to send them out two by two and gave them authority over impure spirits. These were his instructions: "Take nothing for the journey except a staff—no bread, no bag, no money in your belts."

Have everyone recite these verses out loud. Then go around the room again and have everyone try to say them completely from memory.

RESPOND

One of the main takeaways from this session is that God wants us to bring what we have to Jesus and partner with him as he does more than we could ever dream or imagine. Our small offerings can become great in the hands of Jesus. What do you have (such as resources, abilities, time, passions) that you believe Jesus wants you to bring to him? How can your group members pray for you as you seek to offer it to Jesus?

PRAY

Close your group time by praying in any of the following directions:

- Thank God for what he has placed in your care. It could be a few loaves and a couple small fish, but God has placed it in your hands, heart, and life.

- Ask the Holy Spirit to open your eyes to see Jesus and his plan for you. Ask him to open your ears to hear with less and less distraction and noise.
- Lift up your group members and ask God to help them bring what they have to the only one who can multiply it and expand it . . . Jesus.

SESSION THREE

Reflect on the material you have covered in this session by engaging in the following between-session learning resources. Each week, you will begin by reviewing the key verses to memorize for the session. During the next five days, you will have an opportunity to read a portion of Mark, reflect on what you learn, respond by taking action, journal some of your insights, and pray about what God has taught you. Finally, on the last day, you will again review the key verses and reflect on what you have learned for the week.

DAY 15

Memorize: Conclude this week's personal study by again reciting Mark 6:7–8:

> *Calling the Twelve to him, he began to send them out two by two and gave them authority over impure spirits. These were his instructions: "Take nothing for the journey except a staff—no bread, no bag, no money in your belts."*

Now try to say these verses completely from memory.

Reflect: Jesus called his followers to travel light. He did not want them to be weighed down with excess baggage that would distract them from the mission. What represents this kind of "baggage" in your life? What do you need to leave behind that will lighten your load and enable you to follow Jesus more freely?

DAY 16

Read: Mark 6:14–29.

Reflect: John the Baptist followed God faithfully. He pointed people to Jesus and called them to follow the Savior. He rejected the trappings of this world and lived with radical simplicity. He declared with humility that Jesus "must become greater" and that he "must become less" (John 3:30). He was a faithful servant who was imprisoned by King Herod and then executed brutally. How do you respond to the reality that even the most faithful followers of God will often encounter suffering? When have you gone through such a time in your life?

Journal:
- If God is loving and powerful, why would he allow something like this to happen to a faithful servant like John the Baptist?
- How does God use times of sorrow, loss, and pain to deepen our faith and bring glory to himself?

Pray: Surrender your life to follow Jesus and live for him, no matter what comes your way or what happens to you and those you love.

DAY 17

Read: Mark 6:30–56.

Reflect: In this section of Mark, we see Jesus pull away from the crowds so he could get some quiet time with the Father and with his disciples. But the crowds followed him and were there on the opposite shore when Jesus and the disciples landed. Christ was gracious and cared for the masses, even though he was exhausted. He taught, served, healed, and cared for their needs. What can you learn from Jesus' responses to the demands he faced?

Journal:
- How do you tend to respond when you feel the needs of people around you pressing in—but you are also feeling exhausted and in need of refreshment?
- How can you respond more like Jesus and offer care, help, and support to these people—while still making sure your soul stays filled and fresh?

Pray: Ask the Holy Spirit to help you know when you should respond to a need you encounter and when you should make space to rest and care for your own soul.

DAY 18

Read: Mark 7:1–23.

Reflect: In Jesus' day, there were many religious traditions that had been entrenched in the lives of God's people. In some cases, these traditions actually worked against the will of God. The Scriptures said one thing, but the layers and layers of tradition kept people from following them. As a result, many people were honoring God with their lips, but their hearts were far from him. In what ways can believers fall into this same trap today?

Journal:
- What traditions do you follow that could actually get in the way of you walking more closely with Jesus?

• How might your faith become richer if you followed God's Word more and traditions less?

Pray: Ask God to help you embrace those traditions that are rich, meaningful, and biblical but to set aside those traditions that are legalistic and get in the way of you walking intimately with Christ.

DAY 19

Read: Mark 7:24–37.

Reflect: It is difficult to imagine the battle raging inside the heart of this mother. She had watched her daughter be tormented by a demon and longed to see her girl set free. When Jesus saw her faith, he did not put on a show, or use fancy incantations, or even go to the girl's home to bring deliverance. Instead, he simply spoke the word, and the demon ran for the hills. What does this tell you about the authority of Jesus? What does it say about Jesus that he was willing to heal this woman's daughter even though she was "a Greek" (verse 26)?

Journal:
- Where do you see the enemy at work in the lives of people you care about? What is your prayer today for those who are under spiritual attack?
- What are ways you could stand with Jesus against the work of the enemy?

Pray: Lift up praise that Jesus' power over the enemy is absolute and final. Celebrate Jesus' ultimate victory over sin, death, and all of Satan's forces.

DAY 20

Read: Mark 8:1–26.

Reflect: Something strange happens in this story. This is the only time in the Gospels that we witness Jesus healing a person in *stages*. When we read Mark 6–8, it becomes evident that Jesus is addressing both *physical* and *spiritual* deafness and blindness. Jesus was ready to give the deaf hearing and the blind sight, but he also wanted his followers to hear his truth and see his will for their lives. What we learn is that sometimes this is a process. In each of our lives, Jesus patiently works to make us who he wants us to be. Think about how Jesus has been opening your eyes and ears to his will for your life. How can you be more responsive to what the Lord is seeking to do in you and through you?

Journal:
- What tends to get in the way of you hearing and seeing Jesus at work in your life?
- How can you listen more closely for the voice of Jesus and watch for ways he is moving in your life?

Pray: Confess where you have closed your ears and eyes to what God wants to do in your life. Ask for ears to hear, eyes to see, and a heart that is receptive to the will of the Lord.

DAY 21

Memorize: Conclude this week's personal study by again reciting Mark 6:7–8:

> *Calling the Twelve to him, he began to send them out two by two and gave them authority over impure spirits. These were his instructions: "Take nothing for the journey except a staff—no bread, no bag, no money in your belts."*

Now try to say these verses completely from memory.

Reflect: Jesus confronted the disciples over their hard hearts, closed ears, and lack of ability to see. He was not being cruel or mean-spirited in doing so. He longed for each of them to fully experience his presence, see his face, hear his voice, and fall in love with their Savior. He wanted them to leave all their "baggage" behind so they could follow him completely. He wants the same for you today. What has Jesus been calling you to do in recent weeks—but you have been blocking your ears and refusing to respond? How can you grow in faith as you take action on what the Holy Spirit has been nudging and calling you to do?

THE WAY OF THE CROSS

MARK 8:27–10:52

Jesus was consistently clear about what his life would look like. He would serve humbly, die sacrificially, and offer all that he had for our sake. Our Savior was just as specific about what our lives should look like. We are to serve with a joyful and willing spirit, take up the cross every day, and follow him no matter what the cost.

WELCOME

A cursory study of the four Gospels in the Bible reveals that Jesus served humbly, sacrificed willingly, and gave everything for the people he loved. A preview of the early Church shows that the followers of Jesus took this mission seriously. They offered their time, resources, reputations, and even their lives for the sake of the Savior they loved. And this was not true of just the early Church. There have been

Jesus followers throughout history who have counted the cost, took up the cross, and followed Jesus regardless of what came their way.

Richard and Sabina Wurmbrand were two such individuals. The couple came to faith in Jesus Christ and followed him passionately in Communist Romania in the middle 1900s. Richard was tortured for his faith in Christ and spent fourteen years in prison. His wife, Sabina, spent three years in slave labor.

Yet the couple persevered and held fast to their faith. When they were released, they started a ministry called Voice of the Martyrs to help the world learn that many Christians around the world were being persecuted and even killed for their faith in Jesus.

To this very day, Christians have responded to the call to follow Jesus in spite of the cost. Sometimes this means facing rejection. Other times, it can involve the sacrifice of our time and resources as we serve for the glory of Jesus. In many parts of the world, walking in the way of Jesus can still cost a person his or her life.

Jesus modeled a life of sacrificial service and willingness to count the cost. He took up his cross and died for us. Now we walk in his ways—the way of the cross.

SHARE

Think about a person you know who has followed Jesus with bold conviction and counted the cost. What sacrifice has this person made? What have you learned from his or her example?

WATCH

Watch the video for session four. (Play the DVD or see the instructions on the inside front cover on how to access the sessions through streaming.) As you watch, use the following outline to record any thoughts or concepts that stand out to you.

Peter's confession and declaration of Christ (Mark 8:27–30)

A major shift in Mark—from "who is Jesus?" to "what kind of king is Jesus?"

Jesus' first prediction of his death (Mark 8:31–38)

A shock to the twelve disciples—a dead Messiah is a failed Messiah

Peter's rebuke of Jesus and Jesus' rebuke of Peter

Jesus' invitation to humble and sacrificial servanthood

The Transfiguration: glimpses of both suffering and glory (Mark 9:2–13)

Jesus' second prediction of his death (Mark 9:30–37)

The disciples' conversation about greatness and prestige

The way of the cross—the first will be last

The example of a little child (serving those who can't serve us back)

Jesus' third prediction of his death (Mark 10:32–45)

Jesus adds additional details to this prediction

James and John's audacious request

The connection between greatness and sacrifice

DISCUSS

Take a few minutes with your group members to discuss what you just watched and explore these concepts in Scripture. Use the following questions to help guide your discussion.

1. What impacted you the most as you watched Jeff's teaching on Mark 8:27–10:52?

2. If you were to ask people in your community, "Who is Jesus?" what are some of the answers you would get? How would you respond to those same people if they asked you, "Who do *you* think Jesus is?"

3. Read Mark 8:34–36. What did Jesus say is required of those who wish to follow him? What does it mean to "take up your cross" and follow Christ?

4. Read Mark 9:2–13. The Transfiguration gives us a picture of glory and hope in the midst of suffering and service. Why is it important to have a balanced concept of following Jesus that includes *both* humble service and hope in God? What are some ways you keep your eyes focused on the glory of Jesus in the midst of the hard times in life?

5. Read Mark 9:35–37. We are all tempted to seek status and look out for our own interests, but here Jesus calls us to humbly serve others and look out for those who can do nothing to pay us back. What are some practical acts of service that you can offer others (as individuals or as a group) that will reflect the presence and love of Jesus?

6. **Read Mark 10:42–45.** Jesus draws a distinction between the cultural norms of the leaders in his day and the way that his followers should think and live. How did Jesus model what he taught in this passage? How can you follow this call of Jesus?

MEMORIZE

Your memory verses for this week are from Mark 8:34–35:

> *Then he called the crowd to him along with his disciples and said: "Whoever wants to be my disciple must deny themselves and take up their cross and follow me. For whoever wants to save their life will lose it, but whoever loses their life for me and for the gospel will save it."*

Have everyone recite these verses out loud. Then go around the room again and have everyone try to say them completely from memory.

RESPOND

What are some of the service opportunities available through your local church? How could you engage in some fresh new acts of service in partnership with people in your church?

PRAY

Close your group time by praying in any of the following directions:

- Thank Jesus for specific ways he has served you and worked on your behalf.
- Ask for the courage and humility you need to take up your cross daily and follow Jesus boldly.
- Invite the Holy Spirit to show you ways you can serve people who need to see the presence of Jesus.

SESSION FOUR

Reflect on the material you have covered in this session by engaging in the following between-session learning resources. Each week, you will begin by reviewing the key verses to memorize for the session. During the next five days, you will have an opportunity to read a portion of Mark, reflect on what you learn, respond by taking action, journal some of your insights, and pray about what God has taught you. Finally, on the last day, you will again review the key verses and reflect on what you have learned for the week.

DAY 22

Memorize: Conclude this week's personal study by again reciting Mark 8:34–35:

> *Then he called the crowd to him along with his disciples and said: "Whoever wants to be my disciple must deny themselves and take up their cross and follow me. For whoever wants to save their life will lose it, but whoever loses their life for me and for the gospel will save it."*

Now try to say these verses completely from memory.

Reflect: As you memorize this passage, think about how Jesus has served you and sacrificed for you—and what he asks of you in return. What does it mean to take up your cross? What did Jesus mean that those who want to save their life must give it up for the sake of the gospel?

DAY 23

Read: Mark 8:27–9:1.

Reflect: The people of Jesus' day had many opinions about him. The word on the street was that he was someone significant and special. Just think about what people were saying: "Maybe he is John the Baptist, Elijah, or one of the Prophets" (Mark 8:28). All of those individuals were dead—which means one of them would have resurrected! In reality, the people were all shooting too low. Jesus was the *Messiah*, the long-awaited Savior of the world. Today, if Jesus were to ask you, "Who do people say I am," how would you respond?

Journal:

- What are five misconceptions that people in our world today have about Jesus?
- What responses could you provide to clear up some of those misunderstandings?

Pray: Give praise to God for sending his Son, the Messiah, to offer salvation and show us how to live in this world.

DAY 24

Read: Mark 9:2–29.

Reflect: It is hard to imagine what Peter, James, and John experienced on that mountain. They watched as Jesus was transfigured and some of his heavenly glory was revealed. They saw Moses and Elijah, two of the great figures of the Old Testament, with their own eyes. Then they heard the voice of the Father speak to them. Notice that God spoke two things about Jesus and gave one command to the disciples—to "listen to him." What does it look like to "listen to him" in your life? What do you sense God is saying to you today?

Journal:
- What did each part of the Father's declarations—"this is my Son," "whom I love," "listen to him" (Mark 9:7)— say to the disciples who were with Jesus?
- How can you tune into the words of Jesus with greater frequency and attentiveness?

Pray: Ask the Holy Spirit to empower you to follow the words of Jesus you are hearing as you walk through this study.

DAY 25

Read: 9:30–50.

Reflect: As Jesus taught his followers about being last and a servant of all, he pointed them to a child. Children are not powerful, influential, or in a position to reciprocate acts of service. To serve a child is to give without expecting to receive anything back. We are called to serve and give with no strings attached and no quid pro quo. We simply serve because we follow a Savior who served. What is the problem with serving with expectations of reciprocal acts of service or other compensation? What is an act of service you can offer that no one else will see?

Journal:
- Consider the faithful people in your life who have invested in you, served you, and offered what could not be paid back. How have you learned about Jesus through their example?

- Who is one person you believe God wants you to serve with consistency and humility? What can you do to extend Christlike service to this person?

Pray: Thank God for those people who have served you with sacrificial and Christlike care.

DAY 26

Read: Mark 10:1–31.

Reflect: In this story, Jesus encountered a man who was working hard to follow God's commandments. This man thought he was covering all of the bases. But there was one area that was out of line and needed adjusting . . . and Jesus helped the man see it. He was possessed by his possessions. He loved money, stuff, and the material goods of this world. These things had their claws deep into the flesh of his heart. So Jesus suggested that he shift to a generous life free from the control of material things. How did the man respond? He walked away. Why do you think Jesus' command was so difficult for him to follow?

Journal:
- How in your own life have you seen material goods, comfort, and security get in the way of you fully following Christ?
- How do you respond to Jesus' promise of greater rewards to come for those who choose to fully and wholeheartedly follow him?

Pray: Invite your loving heavenly Father to show you what needs to be set aside or put away so you can walk more closely with him.

DAY 27

Read: 10:32–52.

Reflect: To be a Christian means to walk in the footsteps of our Savior and become like him. Jesus himself shows us the way: "For even the Son of Man did not come to be served, but to serve, and to give his life as a ransom for many" (verse 45). When we reflect on the ways that Jesus served as he walked on this earth, we get the picture. When we follow his example, the world can get the picture as well. What does Jesus say is the true path to "greatness"? What do you need to adjust in your life to accurately present this picture to the world?

Journal:

- What are some of the different ways that Jesus served the people in his day—from the disciples, to the crowds, to the people who hated him?
- What could humble service look like in your home, neighborhood, and community?

Pray: Confess where you have focused too much on your desires and preferences. Ask God to help you grow a heart that delights to put others first, just as Jesus did.

DAY 28

Memorize: Conclude this week's personal study by again reciting Mark 8:34–35:

> *Then he called the crowd to him along with his disciples and said: "Whoever wants to be my disciple must deny themselves and take up their cross and follow me. For whoever wants to save their life will lose it, but whoever loses their life for me and for the gospel will save it."*

Now try to say these verses completely from memory.

Reflect: We are all prone to do things our way and protect our lifestyle. But Jesus flips all of this upside-down. The way of Jesus means self-denial, cross-bearing, and willing sacrifice. The people of Jesus' day certainly found this difficult to accept. Why do you think the same is true today—even of those who seek to follow and obey Christ?

PURCHASED BY GOD

MARK 11:1–13:37

As Jesus drew near Jerusalem, he was also coming to the end of his life on earth. In this section of Mark's Gospel, the pace moves even faster and the hatred the religious leaders have toward Jesus becomes more intense. In these accounts of conflict and tension, we find the Savior teaching powerful lessons about who he is and the kind of lives he wants his people to live.

WELCOME

How do you get pure gold? You place it in a crucible and heat it in a furnace. About 2,000 degrees Fahrenheit will get the job done! Intense heat refines gold and makes it valuable.

How do you get a diamond? Three things are needed: pressure, heat, and a master artist. Approximately 725,000 pounds per square inch of pressure are needed to compress the materials, followed by heat ranging from 2,000 to 2,500 degrees Fahrenheit. Finally, the hands of a skilled diamond cutter chisels fifty-eight facets (though this can vary) so that the stone reflects light and reveals the beauty of this unique gem.

Things of rare beauty often demand heat, pressure, and extreme circumstances in their formation. What is true of gold and diamonds can also apply to character and profound truth. It is in the furnace of life and the pressure of adversity that character is forged and truth is revealed.

In Mark 11–13, we find such conflict, tension, and incredible pressure. As Jesus moves toward the city of Jerusalem and the cross, the pace of the Gospel story intensifies and the animosity and attacks of the religious leaders heat up. It is in this furnace that we watch our Savior stand strong and hear his powerful words of wisdom that will shape our lives and character.

SHARE

Think about a pressure situation in your life that helped you become who you are today. How did God use the pressure of that season to shape your character and make you more like Jesus?

WATCH

Watch the video for session five. (Play the DVD or see the instructions on the inside front cover on how to access the sessions through streaming.) As you watch, use the following outline to record any thoughts or concepts that stand out to you.

Sunday:

Jesus' triumphal entry to Jerusalem (Mark 11:1–7)

A dramatic contrast: the crowd's reaction vs. the religious leaders' reaction

Monday:

The fig tree—all leaves and no fruit (Mark 11:12–14, 20–26)

Cleansing the temple—not improving it but replacing it (Mark 11:15–19)

Tuesday:

The conflict intensifies (Mark 11:27–33)

A parable with a pointed message (Mark 12:1–12)

Three questions from the religious leaders:

A question about Roman taxes (Mark 12:13–17)

A question about the resurrection (Mark 12:18–27)

A question about the greatest commandment in Scripture (Mark 12:28–34)

Two powerful challenges:

All leaves and no fruit

Give to God what is God's

DISCUSS

Take a few minutes with your group members to discuss what you just watched and explore these concepts in Scripture. Use the following questions to help guide your discussion.

1. What impacted you the most as you watched Jeff's teaching on Mark 11:1–13:37?

2. **Read Mark 11:15–18.** When Jesus cleansed the temple, he was not simply moving out the animals and money changers but was making a theological declaration. No longer would people come to a *place* to meet with God— now they would draw near to the *person* of Jesus. Why is this so important for believers today? What are some ways you encounter Jesus outside of a formal worship service or church building?

3. **Read Mark 11:12–14 and 20–21.** Jesus was not attacking a tree but was addressing a deep issue in the hearts of religious people. He was saying, "Beware of holding the form of religion while your heart is far from God. Don't be all leaves and no fruit." What is some of the fruit that you

have seen God produce in your life? What helps you to keep your heart passionate and engaged with Jesus?

4. The religious leaders mounted their first attack against Jesus by trying to trip him up with a question about paying taxes (see Mark 12:13–17). However, instead of being tripped up, Jesus called them to "give back to Caesar what is Caesar's and to God what is God's." What does giving "to God what is God's" look like in your life?

5. The second attack from the religious leaders came in the form of a question about marriage after the resurrection (see Mark 12:18–27). Again, Jesus side-stepped their trap and focused on what really mattered—that we belong to God *now*, in this life, but *also* for eternity! How does this bring you hope and confidence as you live for Jesus each day? Why is it important to live with this confidence and hope in the resurrection?

6. The third attack from the religious leaders was about the greatest commandment (see Mark 12:28–31). Again, Jesus focused on what mattered the most—loving God with all of our being. What does it mean for you to love God with all your heart, all your mind, and all your strength? What would it look like in the next week if you were to actively love your neighbor as yourself?

MEMORIZE

Your memory verses for this week are from Mark 12:16–17:

> *They brought the coin, and he asked them, "Whose image is this? And whose inscription?" "Caesar's," they replied. Then Jesus said to them, "Give back to Caesar what is Caesar's and to God what is God's."*

Have everyone recite these verses out loud. Then go around the room again and have everyone try to say them completely from memory.

RESPOND

As you reflect on what you have learned in this section of Mark's Gospel, what practical step could you take to (1) express more consistent and joyful generosity, (2) dare to extend forgiveness to someone who has wronged you, or (3) love a neighbor as you want to be loved?

PRAY

Close your group time by praying in any of the following directions:

- Lift up praises and adoration to Jesus, the King of all kings, who came with humility and glory.
- Ask God to show you where you have "leaves but not enough fruit" in your life. Pray for new fruit to grow as you surrender to his will.
- Pray for the Holy Spirit to grow your love for the Father, who loves you beyond description.

SESSION FIVE

Reflect on the material you have covered in this session by engaging in the following between-session learning resources. Each week, you will begin by reviewing the key verses to memorize for the session. During the next five days, you will have an opportunity to read a portion of Mark, reflect on what you learn, respond by taking action, journal some of your insights, and pray about what God has taught you. Finally, on the last day, you will again review the key verses and reflect on what you have learned for the week.

DAY 29

Memorize: Conclude this week's personal study by again reciting Mark 12:16–17:

> *They brought the coin, and he asked them, "Whose image is this? And whose inscription?" "Caesar's," they replied. Then Jesus said to them, "Give back to Caesar what is Caesar's and to God what is God's."*

Now try to say these verses completely from memory.

Reflect: Each time you read and repeat this exhortation of Jesus, remember that you belong to God and are made in his image. You are to give yourself fully to the One who made you, saved you, and loves you. What are ways you can give yourself to God today?

DAY 30

Read: Mark 11:1–26.

Reflect: Jesus had little patience for religious frills and outward appearances that were a cover for hard hearts and vacant religion. He wanted true relationship, passionate devotion, and fruitful lives. He still does! Dare to take the time today to search your heart and humbly admit where you are just going through religious motions. What is one area you need to get your heart back on track and more in love with Jesus?

Journal:
- What are signs and indicators that your heart is in love with Jesus and your faith is active and fruitful?

- What additional steps can you take to engage your heart more fully with the Savior so that fruit will grow naturally in your life?

Pray: Ask God to show you where the leaves are green but the fruit is withered or gone.

DAY 31

Read: Mark 11:27–12:12.

Reflect: Jesus placed himself and the religious leaders right in the middle of this story. The owner of a vineyard sends his beloved son, the rightful heir, to the tenants of the vineyard to collect some of the fruit. But the tenants, instead of receiving the son with respect and honor, murder him and cast aside his broken body like yesterday's garbage. What comparisons was Jesus making between himself and the religious leaders in this story? What was Jesus attempting to get them to see about the true condition of their hearts before God?

Journal:
- How have you felt the conviction of the Holy Spirit about areas of your life that are out of God's will?
- What can you do to humble yourself and surrender to God's leading in these moments rather than resist and refuse to change?

Pray: Thank God today that he chose to send his Son into this world to redeem you from sin.

DAY 32

Read: Mark 12:13–34.

Reflect: Jesus' object lesson in this story reveals that the first thing we need to give to God is *ourselves*. Once we do this, everything else can follow. When Jesus calls his disciples to give to God what belongs to God, he is reinforcing the call of a disciple. When we call Jesus Lord and commit to follow his will, we are walking the path of discipleship. In what ways are you giving "to God what is God's"? What does this involve in terms of time, dreams, goals, or resources?

Journal:
- What are the parts of your life you tend to hold back and have a hard time releasing to the lordship of Jesus?
- What are some of the consequences that arise when you seek to manage and control those areas of your life rather than hand them over to Christ?

Pray: Pray for strength to take a next step of surrender in one of the areas you journaled about.

DAY 33

Read: Mark 12:35–44.

Reflect: There were times when Jesus was cryptic and subtle about his critique of the religious leaders who were attacking him. There were also times when he took off the gloves and said it like it was. In today's reading, Jesus holds nothing back. He is in the temple courts, and the religious leaders likely thought they had the "homecourt advantage" in this place. What warning does he give to the crowds? What is his main complaint against the religious leaders?

Journal:
- What are signs that a religious leader (pastor, priest, elder, any leader in the church) is being motivated by power, pride, or prestige?
- How should church members pray for and respond to those who are leading them?

Pray: Ask God to draw near to your pastor (or pastors), guide them, and fill them with humility.

DAY 34

Read: Mark 13:1–37.

Reflect: At the end of this section, Jesus gives a warning and an exhortation. The warning is that no person should ever get into a guessing game about when he will return. Jesus did not want his followers hypothesizing about the time of his return. He assures us that the angels don't know, and neither does he. And if *Jesus* himself does not know . . . how could we? Rather, Jesus instructs us to be watchful, vigilant, and always ready. We don't know the time of his return, so we should be prepared at *all* times. What does it look like to live with this kind of hopeful anticipation? What is one way you can be more prepared to meet Jesus?

Journal:
- What are some of the dangers of spending time and energy speculating about when Jesus will return?

- What are some of the advantages and values of actively living in ways that prepare you for when Jesus does return?

Pray: Ask God for discipline and diligence to keep taking the steps that will form a lifestyle that is perpetually ready to meet Jesus when he comes again.

DAY 35

Memorize: Conclude this week's personal study by again reciting Mark 12:16–17:

> They brought the coin, and he asked them, "Whose image is this? And whose inscription?" "Caesar's," they replied. Then Jesus said to them, "Give back to Caesar what is Caesar's and to God what is God's."

Now try to say these verses completely from memory.

Reflect: In the opening chapter of Genesis, we read that "God created mankind in his own image, in the image of God he created them" (Genesis 1:27). How does it impact you to know that you were made in *God's* own image? What do you sense that God is asking you to "give back" to him today when it comes to your time, resources, talents, and service?

A NEW BEGINNING

MARK 14:1–16:20

From his humble birth in a manger, Jesus was the servant king. The closing chapters of Mark reveal God's ultimate act of service for all the world. Jesus was arrested, put through mock trials, beaten, and crucified for our sins. His sacrifice assures us that he was the greatest servant who ever lived. His resurrection confirms that he was—and is—the King of all kings.

WELCOME

We have all heard people use them . . . and most of us have spoken them. They might be uttered intentionally or by accident. They can be humorous and sometimes poignant. They are called *oxymorons*: words or ideas that don't seem to fit together but come right next to each other. Here are some examples of oxymorons that are awfully good:

- Pretty ugly
- Jumbo shrimp
- Good grief
- Crash landing
- Old news
- Open secret
- Deafening silence

The theme of this final session in Mark's Gospel could appear to be an oxymoron. From a human perspective, the words and concepts don't seem as if they belong together. In the eyes of the world, they appear to be contradictory. But these two words go perfectly together in the heart of God and the life of Jesus.

What are these two words? Well, we see them clearly lived out as Jesus went to the cross and rose from the grave. They form a beautiful and powerful oxymoron: *Servant King*!

SHARE

How is Jesus *both* the greatest servant in all history and the most powerful King in all eternity? Why do these fit together in the life of Jesus—even if they sound like an oxymoron?

WATCH

Watch the video for session six. (Play the DVD or see the instructions on the inside front cover on how to access the sessions through streaming.) As you watch, use the following outline to record any thoughts or concepts that stand out to you.

The anointing in Bethany . . . a precious and timely gift (Mark 14:1–9)

Judas turns on Jesus . . . betrayed by a friend (Mark 14:10–11)

The Last Supper (Mark 14:12–31)

    The Passover meal

    Jesus flips the script

The Garden of Gethsemane (Mark 14:32–52)

The trials of Jesus

    The Jewish trial (Mark 14:53–65)

The Roman trial (Mark 15:1–15)

The crucifixion (Mark 15:21–47)

The death of Jesus

The burial of Jesus

The resurrection (Mark 16:1–8)

DISCUSS

Take a few minutes with your group members to discuss what you just watched and explore these concepts in Scripture. Use the following questions to help guide your discussion.

1. What impacted you the most as you watched Jeff's teaching on Mark 14:1–16:20?

2. **Read Mark 14:3–9.** Some of the people at the table were upset at the lavish gift that this woman poured out for Jesus. How was Jesus' perspective dramatically different? What are one or two things you can do today to "lavish" love on Jesus?

3. **Read Mark 14:22–24.** Jesus gave the bread and cup to his disciples. What did these items symbolize? How do you experience the presence and power of Jesus when you partake of communion? (If you have had a particularly meaningful communion experience, please feel free to share it with the group.)

4. Jesus was betrayed by friends, rejected by the crowds, beaten publicly, forced to go through two mock trials, taunted by Roman guards, and separated from his

heavenly Father. He endured physical, emotional, relational, and spiritual wounds beyond comprehension. He did all of this for us. If the amount of willing suffering reveals the depth of love, what does Mark's account teach you about Jesus' love for you? What does it teach you about how Jesus understands the pain you go through in this life?

5. Read and reflect on these three powerful declarations:

When I embrace Jesus as my Savior, I discover that what was done *for* me (by Jesus) is far more significant than what has been done *to* me (by others).

What defines me is not who *excluded* me, but who *included* me.

Jesus picked me out, picked me up, and he will bring me home!

6. Throughout Mark, we see the kingdom of God coming near. In light of all you have learned through this study, what are the ways that Jesus brought the kingdom of God into the world? What are some practical ways you can continue

to bring the power and presence of Jesus into your home, your workplace, your community, and the world?

MEMORIZE

Your memory verses for this week are from Mark 14:23–25:

> *Then he took a cup, and when he had given thanks, he gave it to them, and they all drank from it. "This is my blood of the covenant, which is poured out for many," he said to them. "Truly I tell you, I will not drink again from the fruit of the vine until that day when I drink it new in the kingdom of God."*

Have everyone recite these verses out loud. Then go around the room again and have everyone try to say them completely from memory.

RESPOND

In the opening session, we noted that the Gospel of Mark confronts us with two questions again and again: (1) "Who is Jesus?" and (2) "What does he want?" In this closing section of Mark, we find that Jesus is the *Servant King*, and that he wants us to follow him by giving our lives to others. What is one way you can humbly serve others in the coming week? What is one way you can follow Jesus more closely as you walk through an ordinary day?

PRAY

Close your group time by praying in any of the following directions:

- Pray for courage and a sacrificial heart so that you can give to Jesus with joyful and lavish actions.
- Lift up a prayer in your own words, saying, "Not my will, but yours be done," in areas of your life you have a hard time surrendering to God's will.
- Thank Jesus for experiencing all that humans experience—joy, thankfulness, mercy, as well as sorrow, abandonment, and pain—and ask that you would be tuned in to his presence when you walk through the hard times of life.

SESSION SIX

Reflect on the material you have covered in this session by engaging in the following between-session learning resources. Each week, you will begin by reviewing the key verses to memorize for the session. During the next three days, you will have an opportunity to read a portion of Mark, reflect on what you learn, respond by taking action, journal some of your insights, and pray about what God has taught you. Finally, on the last day, you will again review the key verses and reflect on what you have learned for the week.

DAY 36

Memorize: Conclude this week's personal study by again reciting Mark 14:23–25:

Then he took a cup, and when he had given thanks, he gave it to them, and they all drank from it. "This is my blood of the covenant, which is poured out for many," he said to them. "Truly I tell you, I will not drink again from the fruit of the vine until that day when I drink it new in the kingdom of God."

Now try to say these verses completely from memory.

Reflect: Jesus was willingly poured out. As the eternal King of heaven, he was not a powerless victim. He was a potent servant. Jesus' life blood spilled as he was scourged. It ran down his face as the guards thrust the crown of thorns on his holy head. It flowed as Jesus labored up the hill of Golgotha. His blood poured out as he was nailed to a Roman cross—the Lamb of God who takes away the sins of the world. As you begin memorizing this passage, lean into those words, "poured out for many," and remember that you are part of that host of thankful recipients. How can you pour your life out for the One who willingly emptied himself for you?

DAY 37

Read: Mark 14:1–52.

Reflect: When Jesus was in the Garden of Gethsemane, he uttered some of the most staggering words ever spoken: "Yet not what I will, but what you will" (verse 36). Jesus, the Servant King, surrendered his divine will to the plan of his Father. As we walk in the company of our Savior and follow the way of the cross, these words should be deep in our soul and often on our lips. "Yet not what I will, but what you will." As we begin each day, we should make this declaration, "Yet not what I will, but what you will." When we come to a crossroad or need to make an important decision, our starting point should be to whisper to our Savior, "Yet not what I will, but what you will." How can you let this declaration find a home in your heart and on your lips?

Journal:
- What are examples of times when you have declared or lived with the attitude, "Not your will, but mine be done"? How did it turn out?
- What are two or three areas in which you need to make this declaration—and then live it out day after day? What is a next step you can take?

Pray: Pray these words today again and again: "Not what I will, but what you will."

DAY 38

Read: Mark 14:53–15:20.

Reflect: There is power in a broken and repentant heart. The Spirit of God often whispers and calls us to a place of humble confession. In these moments, holy tears can flow as we mourn our poor decisions. Peter came to such a moment. After publicly denying Jesus three times, a rooster crowed, and he "remembered the word Jesus had spoken to him . . . and he broke down and wept" (verse 72). Something cathartic and liberating is unleashed when we likewise confess, repent, and even weep over our sin. How have you found this to be true in your life? In what ways have you seen God restore you to fellowship after repenting of sin?

Journal:
- How has a time of brokenness moved you to greater intimacy with God?
- How have you made confession and repentance a part of your prayer time with God?

Pray: Ask God to make you aware of any unconfessed sin in your life. Confess those sins to your heavenly Father and ask for his forgiveness and continued leading.

DAY 39

Read: Mark 15:21–16:8.

Reflect: When Jesus was nailed to the cross, he cried out, "My God, my God, why have you forsaken me?" (verse 34). These words come directly from Psalm 22—a prayer of abandonment and anguish as Jesus took the judgment for our sins and bore the shame we deserved. Today, think about the greatness of God's love for you and the sacrifice that Jesus made on your behalf. Remember that Jesus felt *everything* you would have felt on that cross as he paid the price for your sins . . . physically, emotionally, and spiritually. Think about one person in your life who is still carrying the burden of their sin. Commit this week to tell them about the freedom, hope, and life you feel every day because of the sacrifice Jesus made for you.

Journal:
- What are struggles, sorrows, or suffering you are facing right now? What psalms in the Bible might help you as you begin praying through these times?

- How have your burdens been lifted, your sins washed away, and your life been transformed because Jesus died on the cross and rose for you?

Pray: Lift up prayers of praise that the great Servant King, Jesus Christ, gave his life on the cross for you and rose again in glory!

DAY 40

Memorize: Conclude your forty-day personal study by reciting Mark 14:23–25:

> *Then he took a cup, and when he had given thanks, he gave it to them, and they all drank from it. "This is my blood of the covenant, which is poured out for many," he said to them. "Truly I tell you, I will not drink again from the fruit of the vine until that day when I drink it new in the kingdom of God."*

Now try to say these verses completely from memory.

Reflect: As you continue memorizing these words of Jesus, think about the phrase, "Until I drink it new in the kingdom of God." Remember that Jesus is the Servant King and has a kingdom that will last forever and ever. Allow yourself to look forward to the glory of heaven. As you close this study, what images come to mind as you think of that time?

LEADER'S GUIDE

Thank you for your willingness to lead your group through this study! What you have chosen to do is valuable and will make a great difference in the lives of others. The rewards of being a leader are different from those of participating, and we hope that as you lead you will find your own walk with Jesus deepened by this experience.

This study on Mark in the *40 Days Through the Book* series is built around video content and small-group interaction. As the group leader, think of yourself as the host. Your job is to take care of your guests by managing the behind-the-scenes details so that when everyone arrives, they can enjoy their time together. As the leader, your role is not to answer all the questions or reteach the content—the video and study guide will do that work. Your role is to guide the experience and cultivate your group into a teaching community. This will make it a place for members to process, question, and reflect on the teaching.

Before your first meeting, make sure everyone has a copy of the study guide. This will keep everyone on the same page and help the process run more smoothly. If members are unable to purchase the guide, arrange it so they can share with other members. Everyone should feel free to write in his or her study guide and bring it to group every week. Also, make sure the group members are aware that they have access to the videos at any time by following the instructions on the inside front cover.

SETTING UP THE GROUP

Your group will need to determine how long you want to meet each week so you can plan your time accordingly. Generally, most groups like to meet for either sixty minutes or ninety minutes, so you could use one of the following schedules:

SECTION	60 MINUTES	90 MINUTES
WELCOME (members arrive and get settled)	5 minutes	5 minutes
SHARE (discuss one or more of the opening questions for the session)	5 minutes	10 minutes
READ (discuss the questions based on the Scripture reading for the session)	5 minutes	10 minutes
WATCH (watch the video teaching material together and take notes)	15 minutes	15 minutes
DISCUSS (discuss the Bible study questions based on the video teaching)	25 minutes	40 minutes
RESPOND / PRAY (reflect on the key insights, pray together, and dismiss)	5 minutes	10 minutes

As the group leader, you will want to create an environment that encourages sharing and learning. A church sanctuary or formal classroom may not be as ideal as a living room, because those locations can feel formal and less intimate. No matter what setting you choose, provide enough comfortable seating for everyone, and, if possible, arrange the seats in a semicircle so everyone can see the video easily. This will make the transition between the video and group conversation more efficient and natural.

Also, try to get to the meeting site early so you can greet participants as they arrive. Simple refreshments create a welcoming atmosphere and can be a wonderful addition to a group study. Try to take food and pet allergies into account to make your guests as comfortable as possible. You may also want to consider offering childcare to couples with children who want to attend. Finally, be sure your media technology is working properly. Managing these details up front will make the rest of your group experience flow smoothly and provide a welcoming space in which to engage the content of this study on the Gospel of Mark.

STARTING THE GROUP TIME

Once everyone has arrived, it is time to begin the study. Here are some simple tips to make your group time healthy, enjoyable, and effective.

Begin the meeting with a short prayer and remind the group members to put their phones on silent. This is a way to make sure you can all be present with one another and with God. Next, give each person a few minutes to respond to the questions in the "Share" section. This won't require as much time in session one, but beginning in session two, people may need more time to share their insights from their personal studies. Usually, you won't answer the discussion questions yourself, but you should go first with the "Share" questions, answering briefly and with a reasonable amount of transparency.

At the end of session one, invite the group members to complete the "Your 40-Day Journey" for that week. Explain that they can share any insights the following week before the video teaching. Let them know it's not a problem if they can't get to these activities some weeks. It will still be beneficial for them to hear from the other participants in the group.

LEADING THE DISCUSSION TIME

Now that the group is engaged, watch the video and respond with some directed small-group discussion. (Play the DVD or see the instructions on the inside front cover on how to access the sessions through streaming.) Encourage the group members to participate in the discussion, but make sure they know this is not mandatory for the group, so as to not make them feel pressured to come up with an answer. As the discussion progresses, follow up with comments such as, "Tell me more about that," or, "Why did you answer that way?" This will allow the group participants to deepen their reflections and invite a meaningful conversation in a nonthreatening way.

Note that you have been given multiple questions to use in each session, and you do not have to use them all or even follow them in order. Feel free to pick and choose questions based on the needs of your group or how the conversation is flowing. Also, don't be afraid of silence. Offering a question and allowing up to thirty seconds of silence is okay. This space allows people to think about how they want to respond and gives them time to do so.

As group leader, you are the boundary keeper for your group. Do not let anyone (yourself included) dominate the group time. Keep an eye out for group members who might be tempted to "attack" folks they disagree with or try to "fix" those having struggles. These kinds of behaviors can derail a group's momentum, so they need to be steered in a different direction. Model active listening and encourage everyone in your group to do the same. This will make your group time a safe space and create a positive community.

The group discussion leads to a closing time of individual reflection and prayer. Encourage the participants to review what they have learned and write down their thoughts to the "Respond" section. Close by taking a few minutes to pray as directed as a group.

Thank you again for taking the time to lead your group. You are making a difference in the lives of others and having an impact on the kingdom of God!

4⊙ DAYS THROUGH THE BOOK

Study Books of the Bible with Trusted Pastors

The 40 Days Through the Book series has been designed to help believers more actively engage with God's Word. Each study encourages participants to read through one book in the New Testament at least once during the course of 40 days and provides them with:

- A clear understanding of the background and culture in which the book was written,
- Insights into key passages of Scripture, and
- Clear applications and takeaways from the particular book that participants can apply to their lives.

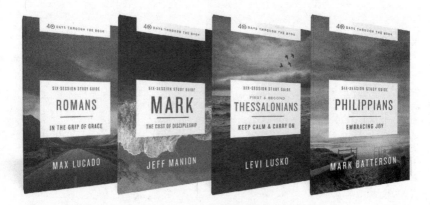

Coming soon to your favorite bookstore,
or streaming video on StudyGateway.com.

Study Guide +
Streaming Video
9780310145998

DVD
9780310129936

MARK

The Cost of Discipleship

Jeff Manion

Who is Jesus and what does it mean to follow him? The focus of Mark's gospel is setting up those questions and answering them. What we find is that he is our servant king who wants us to discover the way of the Christ.

Whether you are exploring the faith for the first time or you have a growing faith over a period of time, Jesus says "Follow Me." Will you join the company of Christ? Will you join our servant king in the mission of expanding the kingdom of God?

— MORE IN THIS SERIES COMING SOON! —

PHILIPPIANS
Embracing Joy

Mark Batterson

Study Guide - 9780310125921
DVD with Free Streaming Access -
9780310125945

THESSALONIANS
Keep Calm & Carry On

Levi Lusko

Study Guide - 9780310127437
DVD with Free Streaming Access -
9780310127451

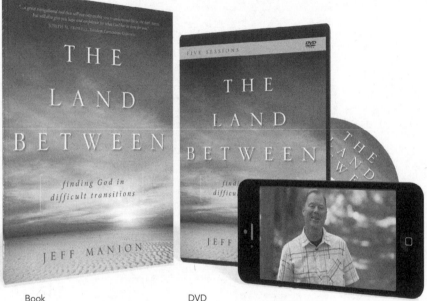